MONSTER ⚙ MACHINES

JETS

DAVID JEFFERIS

D1545224

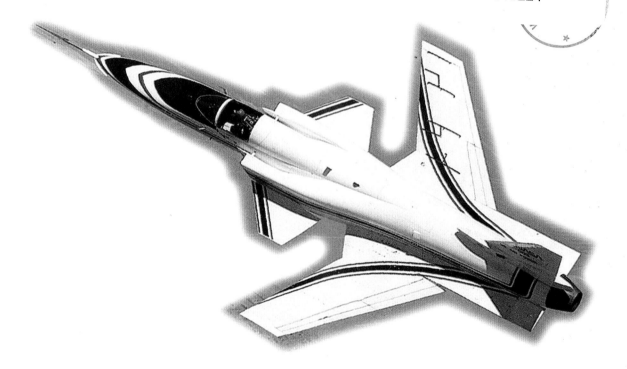

Belitha Press

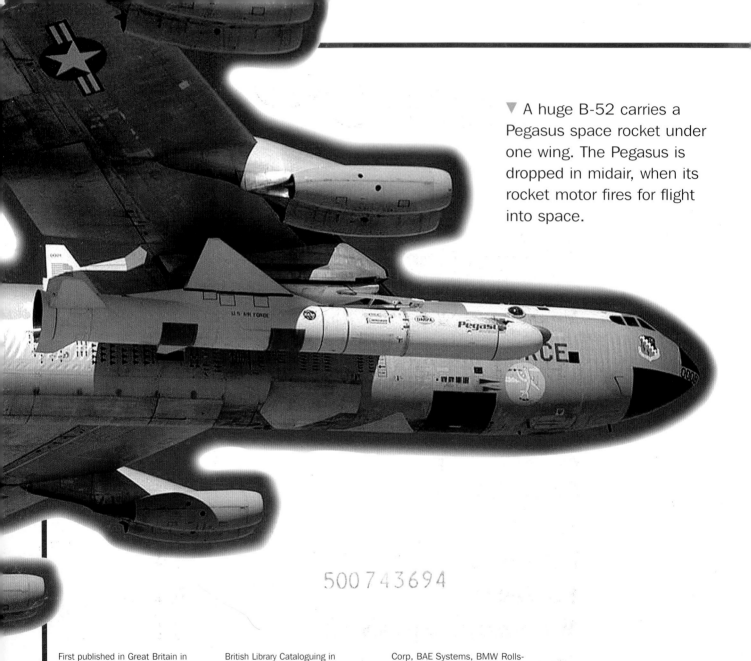

▼ A huge B-52 carries a Pegasus space rocket under one wing. The Pegasus is dropped in midair, when its rocket motor fires for flight into space.

500743694

First published in Great Britain in 2001 by Belitha Press Limited, an imprint of Chrysalis Books plc, 64 Brewery Road, London N7 9NT

Paperback edition first published in 2002

Copyright © David Jefferis 2001

Design and editorial production Alpha Communications
Educational advisor Julie Stapleton
Picture research Kay Rowley

ISBN 1 84138 188 8 (hardback)
ISBN 1 84138 384 8 (paperback)

Printed in Hong Kong.

10 9 8 7 6 5 4 3 2 1 (hardback)
10 9 8 7 6 5 4 3 2 1 (paperback)

British Library Cataloguing in Publication Data for this book is available from the British Library.

Acknowledgements
We wish to thank the following individuals and organizations for their help and assistance and for supplying material in their collections:
Airbus Industrie, Alpha Archive, ANA Airlines, Angel Technologies Corp, BAE Systems, BMW Rolls-Royce AeroEngines, Boeing Corp, Bombardier Aerospace, DASA, Eurofighter, Eurojet, Kawasaki Heavy Industries, Lockheed Martin Corp, NASA Space Agency, Northrop Grumman Corp, Rolls-Royce Plc, Royal Navy, Saab, Scaled Composites, Sukhoi, Teledyne Ryan Corp, TurboUnion Ltd, US Air Force, US Marine Corps, US Navy/Ensign John Gay

CONTENTS

✿ **TECH-TALK**
Look for the cog and blue box for explanations of technical terms.

◉ **EYE-VIEW**
Look for the eye and yellow box for eyewitness accounts.

FLYING BLOWTORCH

The first jets were built as fighters in the Second World War. They were much faster than planes that had propellers.

The Messerschmitt 262 from Germany was the first jet in service. It was a fast flyer for its time, with a top speed of about 870 km/h. The Messerschmitt 262 could be a danger to fly, because its engines caught fire easily. There were many accidents.

▲ The Messerschmitt 262 had two engines, one under each wing.

▼ This jet engine is being tested. In these engines, air is sucked in at the front and mixed with fuel inside. Burning gases roar out of the back and push the plane forward.

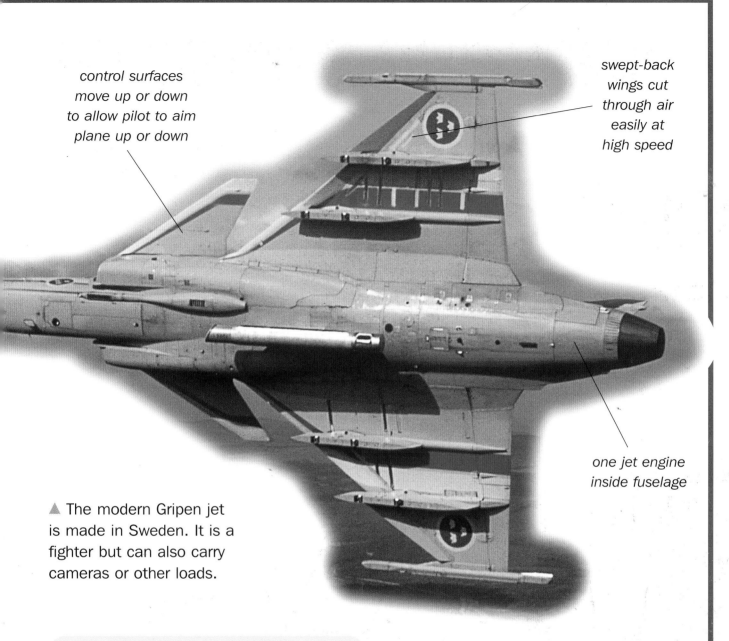

control surfaces move up or down to allow pilot to aim plane up or down

swept-back wings cut through air easily at high speed

one jet engine inside fuselage

▲ The modern Gripen jet is made in Sweden. It is a fighter but can also carry cameras or other loads.

⚙ WHAT IS A JET?

A jet plane is any aircraft that uses a jet engine for power. The 'jet' is really just the blast of high-speed gas coming out of a jet engine's rear. But we often use the word to talk about the whole aircraft. A passenger aircraft that uses jet engines is also called a 'jetliner'.

Today's engines are quiet and powerful. They use less fuel than early models. They hardly ever break down. This is just as well, because many jet planes have only one or two engines. If these fail in flight, the aircraft will crash.

TAKEOFF!

Jet planes have engines to push them forward and wings to lift them up. A plane takes off when it is moving fast along a runway.

▲ The captain and co-pilot's seats are at the front, in the flight deck. It is packed with controls.

As the plane speeds along the runway, air flows quickly past the wings. Air rushing over the curved wing-top is stretched, which creates a low-pressure or suction zone. The effect is like a vacuum cleaner sucking up dust – the plane is lifted into the air.

wings supply lift so jetliner can take off

◄ The Boeing 747 first flew in 1969. It was bigger than any other airliner. The markings on this 747 were designed by Japanese children.

Full engine power is needed for takeoff. A big passenger jetliner has to reach a speed of about 290 km/h before it can leave the ground.

Once the aircraft is climbing safely, engine power can be reduced a little. The plane is then flown smoothly upwards, to its cruising height.

▲ A modern Boeing 777 jetliner next to a propeller airliner of the 1930s, a Boeing 247.

✿ COMPUTERS IN CONTROL?

Many planes are controlled mostly by computers. Airbus jetliners have several computers that control the plane's movements and speed as it flies through the air. An extra computer checks that the others are working properly. Even so, the human captain and co-pilot stay in charge and make sure the computers carry out their orders.

HIGH CRUISE

After the roar of takeoff, the engines settle down to a quieter note. Jet planes cruise high in the sky for most of a flight.

▲ The air is usually calm above the clouds.

At cruising height – about 10 km up – flying is usually smooth. Most clouds, which are bumpy to fly through, are far below. The air outside is cold and thin so the cabin is sealed. Inside, the air is warmed, and pumps keep it thick enough to breathe.

If there is a problem, oxygen masks drop from racks. People can breathe through the masks while the pilot dives lower, where the air is thicker.

▲ The cabins of business jets are usually quite small, but they have comfortable seats and desks so people can work.

▶ The four-engine Airbus A340 is a big jet. It can carry more than 260 passengers at a cruising speed of 870 km/h.

☼ IT'S CHILLY OUTSIDE

When you are sitting comfortably aboard a jetliner, maybe tucking into an in-flight meal, it's hard to believe that just outside your window, the air is very cold. But 10 km above the ground, the temperature of the air is far below zero, at about minus 50°C. Without cabin heating you would freeze to death in a few minutes.

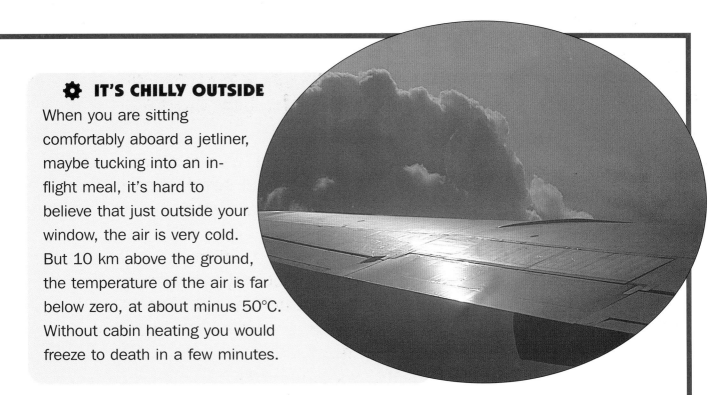

SUPERSONIC FLIGHT

High up in the sky, sound waves travel at about 1062 km/h. A supersonic jet is one that can fly faster than this speed.

▲ The first jet to fly supersonic in level flight was the US F-100.

Concorde is the world's fastest passenger jet. It cruises at twice the speed of sound, known as Mach 2 . Concorde made its first flight in the 1960s. It is the world's only supersonic airliner.

▲ Concorde's nose droops for takeoff and landing. This lets the pilot see forward clearly.

👁 THE BIG WHITE BIRD

'Every time I see Concorde, I think how good-looking it is – like a white swan. Flying on it is old-fashioned in some ways, with a narrow, almost cramped cabin. This has one aisle, with pairs of seats either side. The meals are good though, with specially-prepared food, and the best in fine wines. Mind you, tickets cost much more than those of a normal jetliner!' *Concorde passenger*

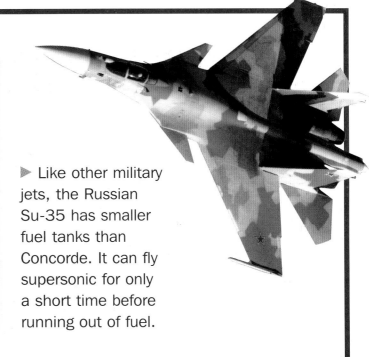

▶ Like other military jets, the Russian Su-35 has smaller fuel tanks than Concorde. It can fly supersonic for only a short time before running out of fuel.

At cruising height, the air is cold, but Concorde flies so fast that its front edges heat up. Hot metal expands, so the jet grows 30 cm longer in flight. It shrinks back to normal as it cools after landing.

Concorde seemed very safe, but in 2000 bits of rubber from a burst tyre set fuel tanks on fire, causing a French plane to crash. This is the first crash in its history.

▼ At high speed, Concorde's nose slides up in front of the flight deck windows, to protect them from heat in flight.

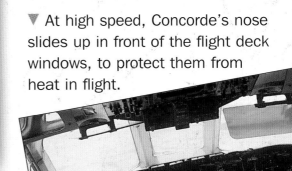

RUNWAY LANDING

The final approach to an airport starts about 30 minutes before landing. Engine power is reduced, the aircraft slows and flies lower.

▲ Pilots line up the plane with the runway when coming in to land.

landing gear is down

In the last few minutes of approach, flaps are lowered behind each wing. Flaps increase lift, but also slow the plane. As the wheels are lowered they make a rumbling noise that you can hear, even in the cabin.

    The pilot heads the plane straight towards the runway. Engine power is adjusted to keep the plane on the correct approach path.

    Then the end of the runway passes underneath, and with a squeal of tyres the aircraft touches down.

▲ The Boeing 777 is one of the biggest two-engine jetliners.

⚙ REVERSE THRUST

Most jetliners have reverse thrust, as well as wheel brakes, to help them come to a halt. Reverse thrust systems have curved parts that jut into the engine exhaust. They channel the exhaust *forward*, so the engine acts as a brake. This makes a roaring noise at touchdown.

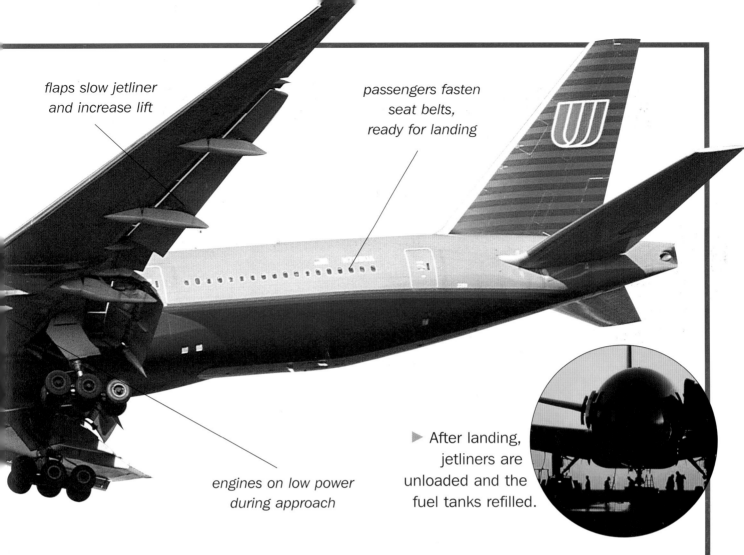

flaps slow jetliner and increase lift

passengers fasten seat belts, ready for landing

engines on low power during approach

▷ After landing, jetliners are unloaded and the fuel tanks refilled.

👁 LANDING AT CITY AIRPORT

'London's City Airport is built in the old docks area. Aircraft have to approach the runway at a steeper angle than normal, and this can seem dramatic, at least for beginners. The first time you land at City, you wonder if your pilot is trying to land the airliner on its nose!' *Passenger*

◁ A plane's path to an airport is tracked by radar. Pilots take landing instructions from staff in a control tower.

SKY GIANTS

Most air cargo is carried in boxes called pallets, which are carried under the passenger decks of airliners. Special jets are needed for bigger loads.

▲ Some jets can drop cargo in flight. Here a C-17 drops food pallets by parachute to starving refugees.

One of the oddest-looking cargo carriers is the Airbus Beluga, named after a type of whale with a large bulge on its head. The Beluga's bulge is where it carries its huge loads. A big door above the flight deck opens up for cargo loading.

AIRBUS INDUSTRIE

▲ The Beluga's flight crew sit below the cargo deck, in a specially lowered cabin in the aircraft's nose.

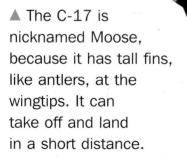

▲ The C-17 is nicknamed Moose, because it has tall fins, like antlers, at the wingtips. It can take off and land in a short distance.

⚙ MOVING ON THE GROUND

The C-17 is built to use rough runways. On the ground the big jet can move in small areas, and can even go backwards, using reverse thrust. It has a ramp at the back for loading cargo. This can be used on the ground, or opened to drop cargo in mid-air.

14

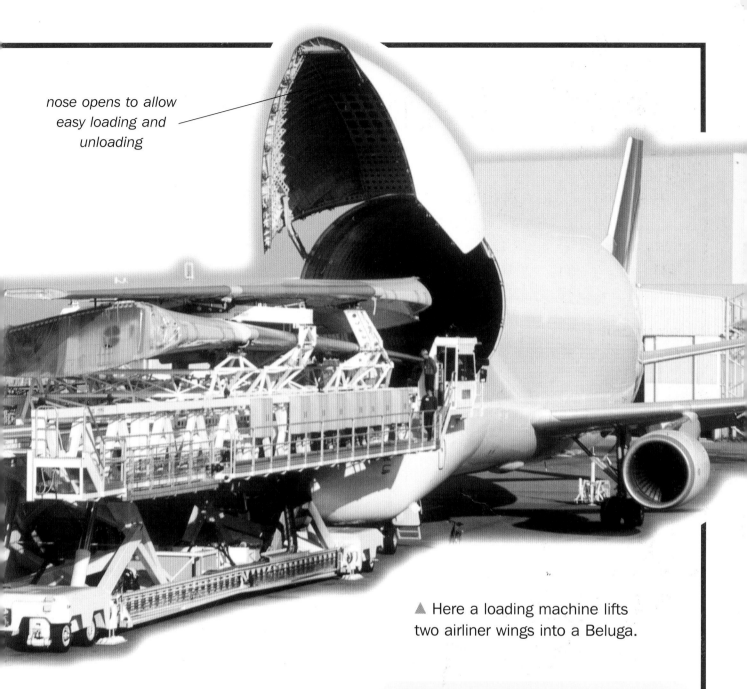

nose opens to allow easy loading and unloading

▲ Here a loading machine lifts two airliner wings into a Beluga.

Although it looks so strange, the twin-jet Beluga is easy to fly. It is used as a flying truck. It mostly carries huge airliner parts between factories around Europe.

The Beluga can swallow a pair of wings, with room to spare.

👁 SEEING THE FLYING WHALE

'We saw the Beluga at the Paris Air Show, and it looked *weird*! It seemed top-heavy and unflyable. Yet computer controls let the pilot fly the Beluga low and slow over the runway, the plane's nose raised high in the air. It was an amazing sight!' *Air show photographer*

JUMP JETS

▲ The X-13 was a small research jump-jet that sat on its tail to take off.

Most jets need long runways for takeoff and landing. However, some can take off straight up. They are called 'jump jets'.

The Harrier is the best known jump jet. It has one engine, with four jet pipes that swivel. They point down for vertical takeoff or landing and to the rear to fly forwards.

fans

▲ The XV-5B used fans in the wings and nose for takeoff.

▼ A Sea Harrier hovers in mid-air. The downward blast from the jet engine keeps it from falling.

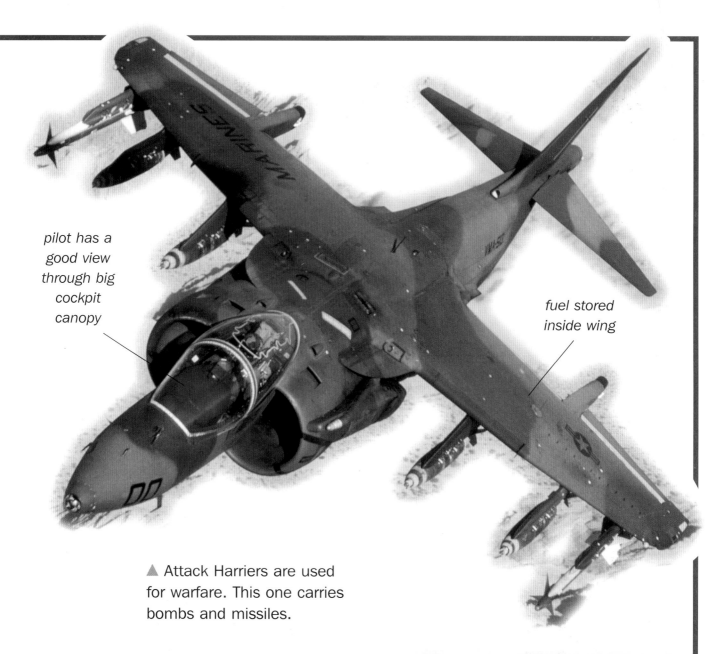

pilot has a good view through big cockpit canopy

fuel stored inside wing

▲ Attack Harriers are used for warfare. This one carries bombs and missiles.

Pilots find the Harrier easy to fly. It has an extra control handle, for turning the jet pipes.

Although the Harrier can take off straight up, it usually makes a short forward run. This means the wings provide some lift, so the aircraft can carry more. After a mission, a Harrier is not so heavy, so it usually lands vertically.

👁 DANCING IN THE AIR

'We saw the Harrier at an air display. It was *very* noisy. It slowed down until it was hovering in front of us. The pilot twirled the plane in a pirouette, dipped its nose in a curtsy, then angled the nose vertical. Then the pilot increased thrust to max, and the little jet shot straight up until it was out of sight!' *Air show visitor*

JET TRAINING

Military jet students go through a long and tough training course when they learn to fly. Only the very best pass their exams and go on to fly combat jets.

▲ A student and instructor get ready for a flying lesson.

▲ Japanese students learn to fly safely in close formation, in T-4 two-seater jets.

Pilots learn how to fly in stages. First they learn to fly propeller planes. Once they have mastered these, they can move on to trainer jets. They have to pass more tests before they are allowed to fly the 'heavy metal' combat machines.

Once they can fly expensive front-line jets, pilots continue to spend much of their time training. This means that they are ready for a real emergency.

⊙ POWER OF A CAT-SHOT

'Hurtling off an aircraft carrier for the first time is *awesome*! You line up your jet on the catapult track, guided by hand-signals from the deck crew, who link a hook to your nosewheel. Inside the ship, the order comes, 'Fire the cat'. With a push on a button the controller sends you off. You get an *incredible* shove in the back – your eyeballs feel like they're going through the back of your skull! Two seconds later, you're in the air and flying at 240 km/h. Wow!' *Student pilot*

▲ Student pilots also learn on electronic flight simulators. Here a pilot practises lining up behind a tanker jet to refuel in mid-air.

▼ The T-45 is a navy jet trainer. Pilots have to be able to land and take off from an aircraft carrier deck. Here a T-45 gets ready for a catapult takeoff.

steam from catapult system

STEALTH JETS

pilot sits in the F-117's nose

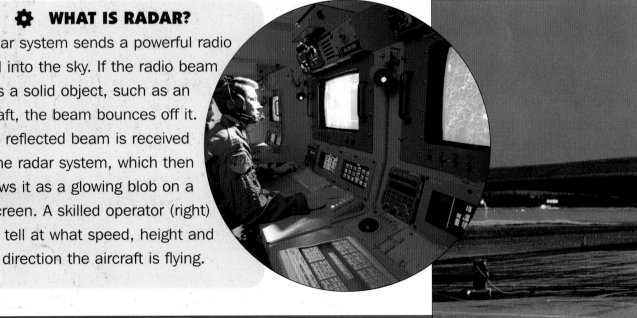

▲ The F-117 stealth jet looks rather like a paper dart.

Stealth jets **are designed to be almost invisible to an enemy's radar defences.**

Radar is an electronic system that can spot aircraft through cloud and at night.

Stealth jets are carefully shaped to reflect signals away from enemy radar. They are also made of special materials that can soak up radar beams.

If a stealth jet flies at night, it cannot be easily spotted either by eye or by radar.

✿ WHAT IS RADAR?

A radar system sends a powerful radio signal into the sky. If the radio beam hits a solid object, such as an aircraft, the beam bounces off it. This reflected beam is received by the radar system, which then shows it as a glowing blob on a TV screen. A skilled operator (right) can tell at what speed, height and direction the aircraft is flying.

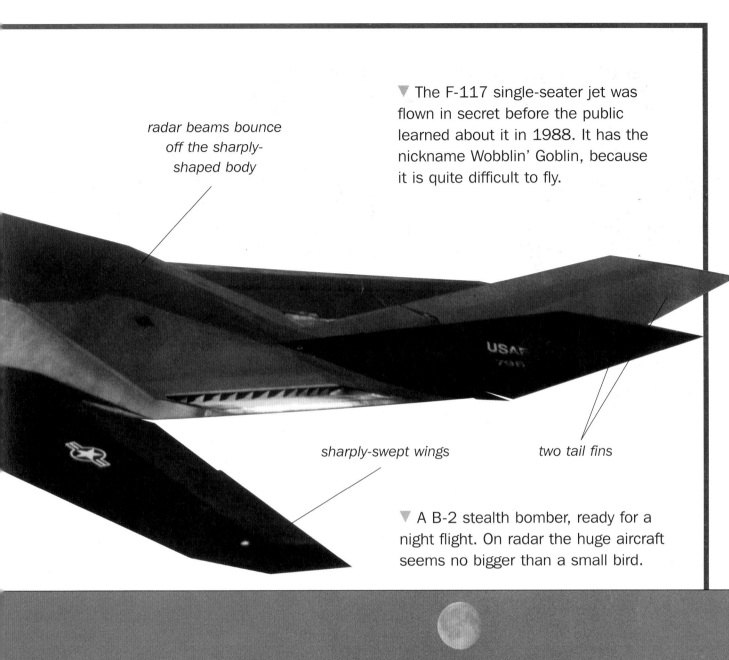

▼ The F-117 single-seater jet was flown in secret before the public learned about it in 1988. It has the nickname Wobblin' Goblin, because it is quite difficult to fly.

radar beams bounce off the sharply-shaped body

sharply-swept wings

two tail fins

▼ A B-2 stealth bomber, ready for a night flight. On radar the huge aircraft seems no bigger than a small bird.

X-JETS

X is for experimental, and jets built for research are among the weirdest-looking aircraft in the sky.

▲ The XB-70 was built in the 1970s. It had six engines and could flash through the air at over 3200 km/h.

The history of flying is packed with oddly-shaped research machines. Here are three of them.

The big XB-70 was designed as a super-speed bomber. New enemy missiles would have been able to shoot it down though, so plans to build lots more were given up after a few flights.

◄ The X-29 was built to test whether a plane with wings swept *forward* could fly. Designers thought the plane would be able to make tighter turns than normal planes.

metal paddles push into jet exhaust to help X-31 turn in tight circles

▲ The X-31 has a single jet engine.
It was built by a US-German team.

The X-29 had forward-swept wings. It flew well, but wings like this are too expensive to make in large numbers.

The X-31 uses three paddles to bend or deflect the jet exhaust. The result is an aircraft that is probably the most nimble flying machine ever made.

👁 **CORKSCREW IN THE SKY**

'Seeing a test pilot show off the X-31 is *amazing*! We saw the X-31 take off, climb straight up, then twist and turn so tightly we thought it must crash. But it flew safely, and through binoculars you could see the jet paddles moving in and out of the exhaust.' *Air show journalist*

FUTURE JETS

Jets of all shapes and sizes will fly in the future, from sleek airliners to insect-like TV-station machines.

The Proteus could be one of the smaller jets of the future. Proteus will fly in circles 15 km high. From here it will beam TV shows to receivers on the ground.

The designers say that Proteus will be cheaper than using space satellites for the same job.

▲ A design for a future jump-jet that could fly from an aircraft carrier.

▲ The Proteus has two sets of wings, and jet engines at the rear.

◄ The Airbus A3XX may seat nearly 600 people on two decks. Despite the huge size, only two crew will be needed to fly it.

A big jet now being designed is the Airbus A3XX. It will be even bigger than Boeing's famous 747 Jumbo. The A3XX will have two decks, with in-flight shops and sleeper cabins for long flights. There are even plans for an exercise gym.

Designers would like to replace Concorde one day. Any new supersonic jetliner would have to be quieter in flight, and use less fuel than Concorde.

▲ Here are some ideas for airliners that might replace Concorde. Designs have not got further than models yet.

⚙ DIFFERENT FUELS AHEAD?

Future jet engines may use different types of fuel. Fuels of today are made of oil. They create pollution and may begin to run out in 20 years. Hydrogen is one possible future fuel. At present it is too dangerous, but there is no shortage of hydrogen, and when it is burnt, the only waste is water vapour.

JET FACTS

▲ Design for a UCAV jet.

Here are some facts and figures from the history of jet flight.

Glider landings

Early MiG jets from Russia had engines that lasted for only about 20 flight hours. To make them last longer, pilots switched off in mid-air and glided in to land.

First jetliner

The first jetliner was the British DH Comet 1, which went into service in 1952.

Lots of money

Jetliners are expensive to buy. A Boeing 747 costs about $180 million!

Close shaves

A jetliner pilot had a narrow escape in 1990. He was sucked out when a flight-deck window broke. One of the cabin crew hung on to his legs, while the co-pilot landed the jet safely.

Talking to a jet

The EFA Typhoon has 'voice input' for the pilot. The jet's computers can recognize up to 200 words, allowing a pilot to give and receive orders. These may be for radio, navigation, or even to fire missiles.

Comfort in the sky

Luxury plans for future jetliners include sleeper cabins, a gym, even a beauty service. One of the best ideas is simple – giving passengers more leg room.

ZH588

▲ The Typhoon is made by companies in several European countries.

Robojets

The next stage in military jet design is the UCAV, or uncrewed combat air vehicle. UCAVs should be able to fly into dangerous areas without risking human pilots. UCAVs should also be cheaper to build and fly than jets with human crews.

High speed

The SR-71 is the world's fastest jet. It made its first flight in the 1960s. Cruising at Mach 3, an SR-71 can fly from New York to London in less than two hours.

Hyper-X

Hyper-X is a 3.7m-long dart-shaped machine designed around a new type of high-speed engine called a scramjet. It will be boosted by the Pegasus rocket (see page 2).

Look, no tail!

The X-36 research jet has no fin or rudder. It has computer controls that

▲ The SR-71 is the fastest military jet ever.

should make them unnecessary. The X-36 is smaller, lighter and cheaper to build than ordinary jets.

Combat best sellers

The US F-16 is the best-selling fighter jet since the 1960s, with sales of more than 4000. In the 1960s more than 5000 F-4s were made. The top-selling military jet ever made is the Russian MiG-21 – more than 15 000 were built.

Farewell propellers

All but the smallest propeller planes are being replaced by jets. In the future, jet engines no

bigger than waste bins may power business and even privately owned planes.

Supercruiser

Supersonic jets normally use an afterburner, which squirts extra fuel into the jet nozzle to give the power boost needed. But the new F-22 can 'supercruise' – it can fly supersonic without an afterburner.

▼ The F-22 is a supercruise fighter.

JET WORDS

cockpit

Here are some technical terms used in this book.

fighter
A jet built for air-to-air combat.

aircraft carrier
A ship that planes take off from and land on at sea.

approach
The path an aircraft takes as it flies towards an airport.

cat-shot
A high-speed launch given by an aircraft carrier's steam-powered catapult.

control surface
The parts of an aircraft used to change direction. Ailerons on the wings roll the jet to the left or right. Flaps droop from the wings to increase lift and drag. Elevators tilt the jet up or down. The rudder controls direction from side-to-side.

control tower
A building at an airport. Staff inside control all takeoffs and landings.

drag
The slowing-down effect of anything that sticks out from a jet. Drooped flaps increase lift as well as drag, so can be used to reduce landing speed.

flight deck
The area at the front of a large jet where the crew sit. In smaller aircraft, the control area is called the cockpit.

flight simulator
A computer-video machine used for training. Pilots practice coping with problems, such as engine failure.

elevator and horizontal stabilizer

fin and rudder

flaps at front and rear of wing

aileron

▼ Control surfaces on a jetliner.

Emirates

fuselage
The main body of an aircraft.

in-flight refuelling
See tanker jet

landing gear
The wheel system used on the ground. Small jets have two main wheels and a smaller nose wheel. A big jetliner may have up to 16 main wheels, with two nosewheels.

lift
The upward motion developed by a wing as it moves forward through the air.

pallet
A specially-shaped box used to carry cargo in jetliners and cargo aircraft. In airliners, cargo pallets are stored underneath the main deck, where the passengers sit.

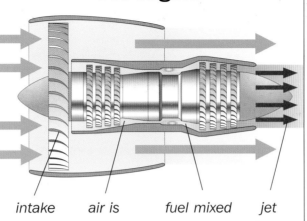

Jet engine

intake fan   *air is compressed*   *fuel mixed in and burnt*   *jet thrust*

The jet engine works by sucking in air with a big fan. Inside the engine, more fans, called turbines, compress (or squash) the air. Fuel is mixed with this air and burnt. Flames roar out of the exhaust, pushing the aircraft forward. Cold air from the big fan also helps push the aircraft forward.

reverse thrust
A system that diverts jet thrust forward instead of to the rear. Used to brake after landing.

supersonic
The speed of sound is called Mach 1. Any speed faster than this is called supersonic. At sea level, planes reach Mach 1 at 1225 km/h. This falls to 1063 km/h higher up.

stealth
A jet, hard to see and designed to be nearly invisible to radar systems.

swept-back wings
Wings that point to the rear. They are used by most jets, as an aircraft with swept wings can slip through the air more easily than with straight wings.

tanker jet
A 'filling station in the sky'. The tanker may have one or more trailing hoses to refuel other jets in mid-air.

UCAV
An aircraft with no humans on board. 'UCAV' stands for uncrewed combat air vehicle.

vertical takeoff
Leaving the ground straight up, without needing a runway. Jump jets have jet nozzles that point down for takeoff, then swing to the rear to go forward.

JETS PROJECTS

These experiments show you some of the science behind the world of flight.

THRUSTING UP

Jump jets work like ordinary jets except that engine thrust can be angled down as well as back. To check the effect, hold a hand shower over the bath. Turn the tap on full to see if this down-force can support the spray.

vary water pressure to change thrust

wave shows up as jet speeds through moist air

BANG POWER

When a supersonic jet passes overhead, you hear a loud bang. This is known as the sonic boom. It is caused by a wave of tightly packed air particles, pushed aside by the plane as it roars along.

1 This project shows the power of sound waves. You need a jar, a metal baking tin, a roll of cling film, a small spoon of sugar and a wooden spoon.

2 Stretch the cling film tightly across the open top of the jar. Wrap the film round the sides firmly. Now sprinkle some sugar grains across the top.

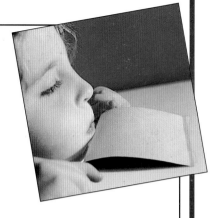

747's wings lift 400 tonnes into the air

LIFT FORCE

Make a wing to see how fast-moving air can create lift. Blowing hard makes a low-pressure area into which the wing is sucked. You need a 10 x 20 cm sheet of paper, sticky tape and a pencil.

1 Fold the paper over to make a wing shape. Tape the ends, and thread a pencil through the front edge. Hold the pencil at each end.

2 Blow hard over the top of the wing. It should lift for as long as you can keep blowing. When you stop, it will sink down again.

3 Hold the baking tin 20-30 cm away and bang it really hard with the wooden spoon. You should see the sugar grains bounce off the cling film as the pressure wave of sound hits them.

distance of storm is one-third of a kilometre for each second delay

SPEED OF SOUND

Knowing the speed of sound can be useful in a thunderstorm. Count the seconds between the lightning flash and the rumble of thunder. Divide the seconds by three to find out how far off the storm is in kilometres.

INDEX